W9-CIG-307

BILL NYE the Science Guy's

GREAT BIG DINOSAUR DIG

With additional
writing by
Ian G. Saunders

Illustrated by
Michael Koelsch

Hyperion Books for Children • New York

Text copyright © 2002 by Bill Nye
Illustrations copyright © 2002 by Michael Koelsch
All Bill Nye photos by Rex Rystedt; pg. 18, dinosaur tracks by Kathleen W. Zoehfeld,
courtesy of Robert T. Bakker; pg. 34, Chicxulub images by William K. Hartmann

For information address Hyperion Books for Children,
114 Fifth Avenue, New York, New York 10011-5690.

Printed in Singapore
Jacket and book design by Angela Corbo Gier

First Edition
1 3 5 7 9 10 8 6 4 2

Library of Congress Cataloging-in-Publication Data on file.

ISBN 0-7868-0542-0 (trade ed.)
ISBN 0-7868-2472-7 (lib. ed.)

Visit www.hyperionchildrensbooks.com

I'd like to thank my parents for my genes; somehow they help me have
a passion for science. But this book is for you. Your genes are just a little
bit different from mine. And, your genes are just a little bit different
from the deoxyribonucleic acid strands in the cells of ancient dinosaurs.
Here's hoping this book helps you know a little bit more about us all
—B. N.

To anyone who ever has ever asked a question and sought its answer, this
book is for you, scientists all. And to scientists past and present: the light
of your curiosity continues to inspire new quests for knowledge, and to
illuminate a future of possibilities
— I. S.

To J. C.
—M. K.

CONTENTS

Rules!

Compsognathus
[Komp-sahg-
NA-thuss]
must have had
a nice smile—
his name means
"pretty jaw."

Introducing
DINOSAURS,
NOW & THEN

Imagine dinosaurs as big as buses walking or wading through your neighborhood. Well, they probably did, but it was long before there were any of us humans here to see them.

Millions of years ago, there were hundreds of dinosaur species on Earth. But something changed in the environment, and all of the big walking, running, scaly-skinned dinosaurs are gone—extinct. That means they died out.

Some of the dinosaurs, a very few, found ways to survive and still thrive today. We now know them as birds. That's right; the birds flying around today are direct descendants of the ancient dinosaurs. In fact, scientists often refer to the ancient dinosaurs as "nonavian [Non AY-vee-uhn] dinosaurs." That just means "dinosaurs that are not birds."

CHECK IT

OUT!

Brachiosaurus [BRAK-ee-uh-
Sorr-uss] was as huge as any
land animal could be, five
stories high and as heavy as
two trailer trucks. Phew.

Paleozoic Era	Mesozoic Era	
540 million years ago	**245** million years ago	**TRIASSIC PERIOD** begins (Age of Dinosaurs begins)

It's hard to imagine just how old ancient dinosaur fossils are.
Follow this time line along the bottom of every page to see how many millions of years it took for you to come into the picture.

The best way to learn about dinosaurs is to dig. We look for fossils. Fossils can be bones, patterns of bones or plants, footprints, or traces of skin. Ancient dinosaur fossils tell us about amazing creatures that once lived on Earth. When we compare dinosaur and plant fossils from ancient times to animals and plants living today, we learn more about how plants and animals fit together in ecosystems. After all, ancient dinosaurs were animals just like you and me. Well, not *exactly* like you and me.

How many people do you know who would gladly eat a whole horse . . . or a few worms?

So You Want to Be a Dinosaur Scientist We call scientists who study dinosaurs "paleontologists" [Pay-lee-en-TAHL-uh-jists]. Paleontology is the study of living things so old that there were no humans around to see or record them. And new discoveries are being made all the time, so paleontology is constantly changing. Until late in the twentieth century, hardly anyone thought birds were dinosaurs. But it sure looks that way now.

TRY THIS!

THE QUESTION:

How did such huge creatures hold themselves up?

HERE'S WHAT YOU NEED:

four bars of modeling clay, about 100 grams (3½ oz.) each
a ½-liter plastic bottle • a 1-liter plastic bottle • a 2-liter plastic bottle
(each bottle should be filled with water and closed with a cap)

1 Take half of one clay bar and cut it in half again. Shape each piece into an upside-down V. Then set the ½-liter bottle on the two Vs, to make a standing "Bottleosaurus."

2 Use a plastic knife or even an old credit card to cut one bar of clay in half the long way to make two pairs of legs about 20 centimeters (8 inches) long. Set the 1-liter bottle on them.

3 Now, use the last two bars of clay to make two big pairs of legs. Using the 2-liter bottle, make an even bigger and heavier model dinosaur that stands twice as high.

DINO #1

DINO #2

DINO #3

As animals get bigger, their legs have to get much thicker. That's why ants can have thin, wiry legs, but rhinoceroses need big, thick ones, like tree trunks. The same is true of animals like you, me, and *Tyrannosauruses.*

How Do We Know
WHAT DINOSAURS LOOKED LIKE?

Well, we don't, exactly.

Plateosaurus [Platt-ee-uh-SORR-uss] got around! His is one of the most commonly found dinosaur fossils in Europe, with discoveries in more than 50 different sites.

No human has ever seen an ancient dinosaur—let alone taken a photo of one or painted one on a cave wall. But we can start figuring out what they looked like by studying their bones and the bones of birds. First of all, dinosaurs had ankles that are different from those of other reptiles. Dinosaur ankles could work like the hinge on a lunch-box lid, just one way. Humans can swing their ankles forward and backward. We can also move them side to side. Well, ancient dinosaurs couldn't do that, and neither can birds.

Scientists also look at animal hip joints. Ancient dinosaurs walked with their legs right under their bodies. So do birds. Other reptiles, like crocodiles, have their legs splayed out at their sides.

Our human hips swivel with a ball in a socket. You can get an idea of how these shapes fit together by clenching the fingers of one hand into a fist. Then hold your fist with your other hand. Your fist is the ball; your other hand is the socket. But in ancient dinosaurs and birds, the hip socket usually has a hole in it. So, it's shaped like a doughnut. Scientists carefully examine dinosaur bones to try to see how all the bones fit together.

Assembling bones from a fossil dig into a dinosaur skeleton is just like putting a jigsaw puzzle together. Well, it's not quite so easy. Dinosaurs weren't flat; they had muscles and skin, which we can't see. And there's no picture on the box to show you what the dinosaur is supposed to look like when you're done!

By building dinosaur skeletons, scientists get a pretty good idea of how tall dinosaurs were, whether they stood on two or four feet, and about how big their brains were compared to their bodies.

Camouflage Most animals have coloring that helps them blend in with their surroundings. This coloring, called camouflage [KAM-uh-Flahzh], helps animals hide from predators or sneak up on their prey. We see masked raccoons, striped zebras, patchy and splotched whales, and snakes with patterns like international flags. So it could be that ancient dinosaurs had wild patterns and colors as well. What do you think?

SKIN QUIZ OF SCIENCE

A   B   C

Stripes, splotches, and holding still can all help an animal hide.

CHECK IT **OUT!**

In 1842, Richard Owen made up the word *dinosaur*, meaning "fearfully big lizard."

C Snake
B Leopard
A Zebra

TRY THIS!

THE QUESTION:

How did dinosaurs use camouflage to hide?

HERE'S WHAT YOU NEED:

a balloon (try a green or tan one) • tempera paints
a place to hide (like the woods, a sandy area, or your backyard)

1 Blow up your balloon and pretend it's a dinosaur
(a Balloonosaurus?).

2 Decide what kind of environment your Balloonosaurus
lives in. The woods? The grass? A sandy desert?
Or perhaps on a barren rocky slope?

3 Paint your Balloonosaurus to blend into your environment.
Try brown, green, yellow, and black splotches for a forest.
If you want to hide in dry grass, try tan and black stripes,
like a tiger.

Camouflage isn't perfect, but it doesn't have to be.
After you get a pattern worked out, see if a friend can
find your Balloonosaurus in, say, a minute.
That's plenty of time for an animal to
plan an escape or an attack.

FORMING A FOSSIL

Pachycephalo-saurus [Pak-ee-SEFF-uh-luh-Sorr-uss] was a real blockhead. He had a head like a dome with a very thick skull, up to 25 centimeters (10 inches) thick!

Fossils provide evidence that ancient dinosaurs once lived. Most fossils were formed when animals died and got buried by earth that was moved by winds or floods. When the buried animals and the soil around them got very wet, minerals in the soil worked their way into the bones. Sometimes, chemical reactions changed the composition of the bones, making them as hard as rocks, and preserving the tiny details of the bone shapes. We call this "permineralization" [per-MIN-(uh)-ril-ih-Zay-shun].

If the conditions are just right, the permineralized bones are not dissolved away as they lie in the ground, and the loose soil and sand that once surrounded the bones harden into rock. Since the bones are still inside, the animal or trace of animal is preserved within the solid rock.

Paleontologists have learned how to look for rocks that might hold fossils. They usually find one edge or end of a bone, then start digging into the earth around that spot. In general, things that are buried at the same depth in a layer of rock or dirt are about the same age. To get to most fossils, scientists have to chip away very carefully at solid rocks. Phew.

CHECK IT **OUT!**

People have been digging up fossils for centuries. Thousands of years ago, Greek people found fossils of giraffes that had gone extinct millions of years earlier. But our modern dinosaur digging really took off when scientists in Europe started to find bones and teeth of large mysterious reptiles in the early 1800s.

TRY THIS!

THE QUESTION:

How do bones become permineralized?

HERE'S WHAT YOU NEED:

an old sponge • salt • a big glass of warm water • a spoon • a saucer

1 Add 50 milliliters (3 tablespoons) of salt to the glass of warm water. Stir it until most of the salt disappears.

2 Soak your sponge in this salty, salty water. Squeeze and resoak the sponge to work the salty water all the way through.

3 Tip the glass and gently drain away the excess water.

4 Slide your permineralized salt sponge onto the plate and let it dry for a few days. If you want, you can bury it in some sand, and let it dry there like a fossil bone in the earth.

When you pick it up (or dig it up), you can feel that it's solid and stiff as a rock. Look at it closely in bright light, and you'll see sparkly mineral crystals.

Your sponge has become "permineralized"— a lot like a fossil dinosaur bone.

Digging Up BONES

Tyrannosaurus rex [tih-RAN-ih-Sorr-uss] had teeth as much as 23 centimeters (9 inches) long and could eat 1/4 ton in one bite!

In general, places that are wet today don't hold many dinosaur fossils. The flow of water is always shifting things around, carrying them away, and dissolving them for good. Fossils are preserved when they are buried in soil that can withstand sun and rain for millions of years.

Animals hang out where there's water to drink and plants to eat. So, when we go looking for fossils, we often look in places where there used to be water—ancient riverbeds, gorges, gulches, or canyons that have dried out.

By looking closely at dinosaur bones, we can come up with theories about their behavior. For example, many *Tyrannosaurus* skeletons have been found with healed broken ribs. And from their skeletons, we also know that they had very short arms. A few scientists figured that if a *Tyrannosaurus* fell down, he could get badly hurt, because he couldn't break his fall by extending an arm as, say, a human can. So it could be that they didn't run any faster than the speed at which they could safely fall.

This is just one possible explanation for the cracked rib bones in the rocks. What do you think?

CHECK IT **OUT!**

The material encasing a fossil is called the "matrix" [MAY-tricks]. The rock or soil you have to dig down through to get to a fossil is called the "overburden."

TRY THIS!

THE QUESTION:

How do you get a fossil out of a rock without damaging it?

HERE'S WHAT YOU NEED:

a chicken bone or two • plaster of Paris • 2 paper buckets or large paper cups • old toothbrush • safety glasses

1 Next time you eat a piece of chicken, save a bone or two. Then clean the meat off of them and let them dry for a few days.

2 Mix up the plaster of Paris in one of the cups. Pour about half of the mixture into the other cup.

3 Set the bone(s) in the plaster of the second cup; then cover it up to the top with the rest of the plaster. You could also have a friend set the bone(s) in the plaster, so you don't know exactly where it is in the bucket.

4 Let the plaster harden for several hours or, better yet, a couple of days.

5 Peel the bucket away and then see how easy (uh, difficult) it is to get a fossil out of a rock. You may have to use a hammer and chisel. Protect your eyes with safety glasses if you do. If you don't have a chisel, try a rock that has a sharp edge.

To remove the bone cleanly, you have to scrape the plaster off and then, very carefully, brush it away using the toothbrush.

Seismosaurus
[SIZE-muh-
Sorr-uss] was
one of the
longest land
animals that
has ever existed,
at 40–50 meters
(130–170 feet).

Making Tracks

Not all dinosaur fossils are bones. Scientists have found dinosaur tracks and traces of dinosaurs' digestive systems and respiratory tracts (breathing tubes and lungs).

Dinosaur tracks help us answer a whole new set of questions: How much did she weigh? Did he walk on two feet or four? Did she drag her tail when she ran? We look at the depth of the prints and the spacing between prints. We can also look closely at how deeply the toes or heels dug in to understand if the dinosaur was hurrying or strolling through some ancient muddy spot.

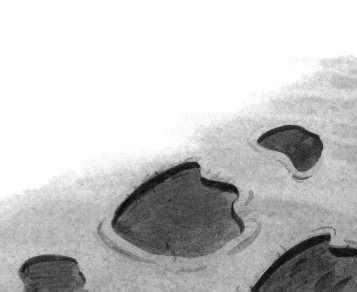

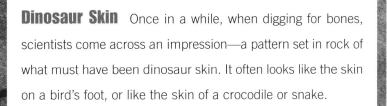

Dinosaur Skin Once in a while, when digging for bones, scientists come across an impression—a pattern set in rock of what must have been dinosaur skin. It often looks like the skin on a bird's foot, or like the skin of a crocodile or snake.

We find dinosaur tracks all around the world. They were formed when animals walked through mud, maybe near a swamp or bog. Then the whole area had to dry out before the prints were wiped away by weather, like rain. And the dried-out rocky area has to be where humans can stumble upon them millions of years later.

Think about walking through a muddy spot near where you live. How long do you think it would be before someone or something else came through and destroyed the impressions you had left? Probably not long. Unlikely as it may seem, there are many places in the world where we've found dinosaur "trackways," places where ancient dinosaurs left footprints. Trackways are usually in deserts, places that are now very, very dry, but were once part of completely different ecosystems.

CHECKIT

OUT!

We can go see the tracks of a giant herbivore in Texas. Right alongside them there are the tracks of a smaller carnivore. Maybe the meat-seeker was hunting the big plant-chewer. We can't tell exactly what happened; but like each fossil we find, every trackway tells a story.

TRY THIS!

THE QUESTION:
What do we learn from dinosaur trackways?

HERE'S WHAT YOU NEED:
a long roll of paper (about 5 meters, or 15 feet)
tempera paint any color • an old baking pan or dish

1 Roll the paper out on a lawn or sidewalk.

2 Pour some paint in the dish.

3 Take off your shoes and socks, step in the dish, then walk on the paper. Try running, walking on your hands, or crab walking, with your stomach up and hands behind you.

4 To study it later, hang it on your wall.

By looking at the patterns of your trackways, you can tell how you or your friends (Humanosauruses?) were getting around, and how quickly. That's what scientists do with trackways.

Ankylosaurus [ang-KYLE-uh-Sorr-uss] had great built-in protection from his predators, with thick, armorlike skin, large horns on the back of his head, and a clublike tail.

Short, Tall, *Fast,* & SLOW—

They Were Everywhere, You Know!

Every year, scientists unearth fossils of new ancient dinosaurs. We find about seven new species each year. They came in all shapes and sizes, like the animals of today—though there aren't any land animals today nearly as big as even the medium-size ancient dinosaurs. A *Seismosaurus* [SIZE-muh-Sorr-uss] weighed as much as ten elephants. But the largest animals that have ever lived on Earth are still around today—blue whales. They can get as big as they are because their bodies are supported by water.

146
million years ago
CRETACEOUS PERIOD *begins* • *Allosaurus* • *Apatosaurs (Brontosaurus)*

Dinosaurs are divided into two groups, depending on their hip structure.

SAURISCHIANS

One group had hips like lizards. The big hip-bone called the "pubis" [PYOO-biss] went forward. We call these dinosaurs saurischians [Sorr-ISH-ee-inz], meaning "lizard-hipped."

Scientists further divide the saurischians into two groups, depending on the type of feet they had.

Sauropods [SORR-uh-Pahdz] had "lizard feet."

Theropods [THAIR-uh-Pahdz] had "beast feet." Their feet were fitted with big, sharp claws. These theropods are the ancestors of the birds we see flying and running around today.

ORNITHISCHIANS

The other group of dinosaurs had hips that made early scientists think of birds. We call them "ornithischians" [Or-nih-THISH-ee-inz], "bird-hipped," even though they didn't turn out to be the ancestors of birds. Their pubis bones pointed backward.

> Birds did not actually come from what early paleontologists called the bird-hipped dinosaurs. That's the way science goes sometimes.

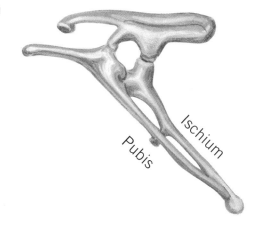

SAURISCHIAN

Ischium

Pubis

ORNITHISCHIAN

Ischium

Pubis

Warm-blooded, Cold-blooded, or Both? You and I are what we call "warm-blooded." We keep the same body temperature all day. Being warm-blooded allows us to move pretty fast, even when it's cold out. Modern reptiles are what we call "cold-blooded." Their body temperatures go up and down with the temperature of their surroundings. So, it takes time for a cold-blooded animal to rev up after a cool night.

Scientists are still debating whether the ancient dinosaurs were cold-blooded or warm-blooded. Birds are warm-blooded, so it would make sense that dinosaurs were as well. But, on the other hand, reptiles are cold-blooded, and dinosaurs had a lot in common with them, too. Maybe you'll be the scientist who figures it out.

CHECK IT

OUT!

On Earth right now, there are also animals that show characteristics of being both warm-blooded and cold-blooded. Leatherback sea turtles (which are reptiles) keep the same temperature all the time. And African naked mole-rats (which are mammals) let their body temperature go way down at night. So maybe some dinosaurs were warm-blooded and others were cold-blooded.

IT'S TIME TO PLAY . . .
"WHAT'S MY BODY TEMPERATURE?"

WARM   COLD   ?

TRY THIS!

THE QUESTION:
What does it mean to be warm-blooded?

HERE'S WHAT YOU NEED:
a thermometer • a shower or bathtub

1 Measure the temperature inside your body with a thermometer under your tongue. For most of us, it's about 37.0 degrees Celsius (98.6 degrees Fahrenheit).

2 Now, take a cold shower for a couple of minutes. You'll feel cold when the water hits your chest, your "core." Then, measure your body temperature again.

3 Now, take a hot shower, or get in a hot bath. Measure your temperature.

4 Try running around until you're hot and sweaty. What's your temperature now?

Although your skin temperature changes a bit, your inside body temperature stays the same. You're warm-blooded.

WHAT'S FOR DINNER?

Iguanodon [ih-GWAN-uh-dahn] earned his name by having teeth that are similar to those of an iguana. Ancient dinosaurs had to eat, just like you and me.

If you think about it, figuring out what an animal likes to eat tells a lot about his or her behavior. Scientists like to divide animals into three categories, according to what they eat: meat eaters, plant eaters, or some-of-each–eaters. We call them carnivores [KAR-nih-vorz], herbivores [HERB-ih-vorz], and omnivores [AHM-nih-vorz]. You may have eaten Mexican pork strips called *carnitas.* Then you're a meat eater. Or you may have enjoyed food seasoned with bits of leaves or "herbs." Then you're a plant eater. Most humans eat both meat and plants. We're omnivores. In Latin, *omni* means "all" or "everything."

125
million years ago   *Utahraptor*

We can figure out what ancient dinosaurs must have eaten by taking a close look at their teeth. Carnivores have long, sharp, tearing teeth. Herbivores can have sharp, scissorlike teeth in the front and flat teeth with low tough ridges for grinding plants in the back.

Inspect a cat's choppers, and you'll find carnivorous [Kar-NIH-ver-uss] teeth. Check behind a cow's lips and you'll see herbivorous [Hir-BIH-ver-uss] grinder teeth. Open your mouth in front of the mirror, and you'll find that you have sharp teeth in front and low, strong grinding teeth in back.

JURASSIC SPECIALS

FOR HERBIVORES
SAUTÉED FERNS IN A DELICATE
RIVER-WATER SAUCE

FOR OMNIVORES
SAUTÉED FERNS OR ANY
NEIGHBORING ANIMAL

FOR CARNIVORES
ANY DINOSAUR AT YOUR TABLE
(PLEASE DON'T EAT YOUR
WAITER!)

The majority of animals, now and in ancient times, eat plants. These herbivores need lots and lots of plants to feed on. Carnivores usually eat herbivores. If there are too many carnivores in an ecosystem, pretty soon there isn't enough food to go around. Scientists often think of ecosystems as being a food pyramid with tons and tons of plants at the bottom, plenty of herbivores in the middle, then just a few meat-eating predators at the top.

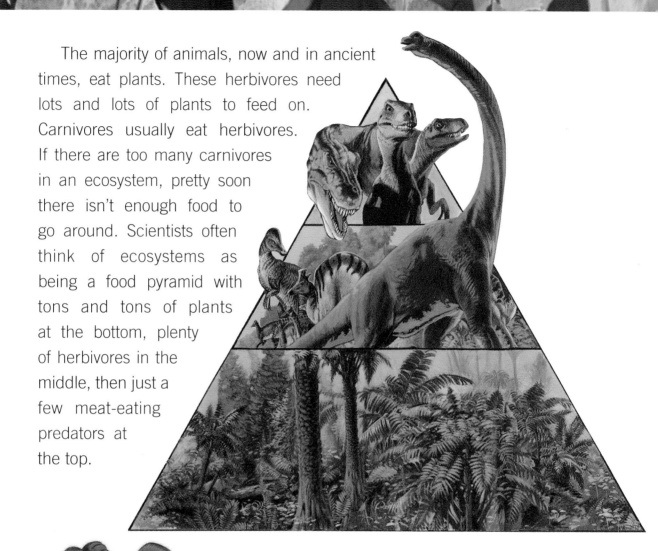

Raptors Animals with big claws or talons [**TAL-unz**] are often called "raptors" [**RAP-torz**]. That means "robbers" in Latin. Nowadays the only living raptors are birds. What do animals do with talons? Well, they catch animals and eat them. If you eat plants, you don't have the problem of your food running away. So, when scientists found the bones of what must have been a very fast-running carnivore, they called it *"Velociraptor"* [**veh-LAHSS-ih-Rapp-ter**], a raptor with velocity, or speed.

TRY THIS!

THE QUESTION:

Are you a carnivore, herbivore, or omnivore?

HERE'S WHAT YOU NEED:

meat foods • vegetable foods

1 Try eating only meat for a whole day. Have, say, sausage or bacon for breakfast, bologna for lunch, and chicken for dinner. That means no bread, no potato chips, no pickles or lettuce, mustard, or ketchup for a whole day. You'll probably find yourself hankering for some crunchy celery or smooth peanut butter before long.

2 Try eating only vegetables for a day. Have peas, carrots, spinach, beans, and potato chips. To be a real herbivore, you shouldn't have any milk, cheese, or fish. Those all come from animals.

What are you?

Time, Time, more TIME

Your parents might be about thirty years older than you are. Your grandparents might be about sixty years older than you are. But the fossils of the ancient dinosaurs are 65 million years older than anyone alive today.

Dinosaurs started living on the earth about 230 million years ago, and most of them died out 65 million years ago. We figured this out by careful, careful study of the rocks in which dinosaur fossil bones were found. There are a few different ways that scientists can figure out how old dinosaur fossils are.

Over time, rocks on the Earth's surface pile up in layers. Scientists call each layer of rock a "stratum" [STRAT-uhm]; multiple layers are called "strata" [STRAT-uh]. By looking at the type of rock, where it is on the Earth's surface, and the thickness of each stratum, scientists figure out how old the layers are. If you find a fossil in a particular stratum, then you know about how old it is. This is the oldest (and still very good) way to date fossils. We call the study of strata "stratigraphy" [stra-TIG-ruh-fee]. Usually, the deeper a fossil is buried, the longer it's been there.

Another method of dating fossils is studying the rocks in which they are found. Rocks have many different minerals in them, one of which is potassium [poh-TASS-ee-um]. It's made of tiny particles called atoms [AT-umz]. Each potassium atom has nineteen almost unimaginably even tinier particles inside it called protons [PRO-tahnz]. As these atoms age, they lose a proton, ending up with only eighteen. Then, they become a completely different substance called argon [AR-gahn].

106 million years ago *Dinosaurs thrive in what is now Antarctica*

Many dinosaur fossils are buried under the ash of volcanoes that erupted millions of years ago. After the ash is tossed up onto the surface from Earth's core, the potassium atoms in the ash slowly decay and change into argon. Scientists have learned to predict how long it takes for this to happen. By carefully measuring how much potassium and argon are in the soil around fossils, we can calculate how long ago a fossil was buried. By the way, volcanoes are still erupting today, and once in a while, plants and animals are buried. They might someday become fossils, too.

Radioactive minerals inside the Earth help us date fossils.

Deinonychus • Giganotosaurus

Eras and Periods Scientists who study the Earth, who are called geologists [Jee-ahL-uh-jists], have figured out that our planet has gone through different ages of time. The first block of time is called the Paleozoic [Pay-lee-uh-ZOH-ik] Era, or "ancient time." But the ancient dinosaurs lived in what's called the Mesozoic [MEZ-uh-Zoh-ik] Era, the "middle time." We live in the era after the Mesozoic, called the Cenozoic [Sen-uh-ZOH-ic] Era. It means "recent time."

After carefully studying the layers of rock and soil in the Earth's crust, geologists have gone on to subdivide the Mesozoic Era into three smaller periods: First was the Triassic [try-ASS-ik] Period, which was the time when dinosaurs first appeared. Then, there was the Jurassic [jer-ASS-ik] Period, which occurred in the middle of the Mesozoic Era. It's named after the Jura mountains in Europe, where the layers of rock from this period were discovered. The latest or more recent period was the Cretaceous [krih-TAY-shiss]. That means chalky; it was first understood by studying chalky rocks. Different kinds of dinosaurs lived during all three periods of the Mesozoic Era.

EARTH'S CRUST

CENOZOIC →

Cretaceous →

MESOZOIC — Jurassic →

Triassic →

PALEOZOIC →

CHECK IT

OUT!

Many dinosaurs never saw a flower or bit into fruit from a tree. There were no flowers until the Cretaceous Period. Before that, it was all ferns, ferns, ferns.

TRY THIS!

THE QUESTION:

How much time has passed since dinosaurs were around?

HERE'S WHAT YOU NEED:

a 500-sheet package of paper • drawing pencils, markers, or crayons

1 Write "*Giganotosaurus*" [jie-gan-NAH-tuh-Sorr-uss] at the very top of the first page of the stack of paper. That's the start of your Pages of Time. The stack of paper represents 100 million years. Each side of each page represents 100,000 years.

2 The ancient dinosaurs became extinct 65 million years ago. You can mark that 175 pages after Giganotosaurus.

3 Now, go to the bottom of the back of the very last sheet of paper. That's where we come in. The last Ice Age ended about 25,000 years ago. That would be a fourth of the way down the back of the last page. Fold the paper there and mark it. The pyramids in Egypt were built around five thousand years ago. Mark that on the same page just 14 millimeters (⁹⁄₁₆ inch) from the bottom. Almost all of human recorded history—every newspaper, movie, photograph, king, queen, president, and actor lived below this line. So do you and I.

4 If you live to be 90 years old, your whole life will fit in a pencil line just 0.25 millimeter (¹⁄₁₀₀ inch) wide right on the bottom edge of the back of the last page.

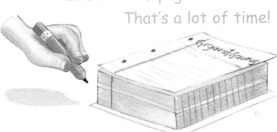

That's a lot of pages.
That's a lot of time!

Where Did
All the Ancient Dinosaurs Go?

You and I are surrounded by living things. And every living thing affects the others around it. Ancient dinosaurs lived in the same kind of world. But 65 million years ago, something happened that made almost all the dinosaurs disappear. For a long time, scientists have reasoned that most of these magnificent animals must have stopped fitting into their changing environment. They may have been slowly disappearing by the end of the Mesozoic Era.

But until the mid-1980s, no one had a good theory, or idea, of how so many of the dinosaurs could have disappeared at once. Now, many scientists agree that the ancient dinosaurs were killed by meteors, or rocks, from outer space. They figured this out by looking not only at fossils but also at the rocks and soil in which they were buried.

Wherever we find fossils from the last dinosaurs of 65 million years ago, we also find a layer of unusual metal. It's shiny like silver, and it doesn't rust. Similar to chromium (which makes chrome car parts shiny), it's called iridium [ih-RIH-dee-um]. On Earth it is quite rare, but it's pretty common in rocks that have fallen from outer space.

At about the same time that Earth and the other planets were formed by gravity pulling particles of stardust together, much smaller bits of rock and ice

75
million years ago   *Corythosaurus*

also formed. (When I say smaller, I mean anywhere from the size of a speck of dust to the size of a city!) When these rocks slam into Earth's atmosphere and trail a bright streak through the sky, we call them meteors [MEE-tee-urz]. If they make it all the way to the ground or the sea, we call them "meteorites" [MEE-tee-ur-Ites].

Sixty-five million years ago, a meteorite or group of meteorites about 15 kilometers (10 miles) across came slamming into Earth from outer space. Traveling very fast, at least 11 kilometers per second (almost 40,000 kilometers per hour), they hit the ground with a lot of energy. That energy had to go somewhere, so it probably caused a huge explosion, a fireball of molten (melted) rock. The force of the wind alone would have blown animals and trees right over. The flying debris became a worldwide dust cloud. When the dust settled, it left a layer of iridium all over the place. Now, scientists find a layer of iridium buried just above the layer containing the last of the Cretaceous dinosaurs.

With all that smoke and dust in the air, light and heat from the Sun were probably reflected back into space. So green plants that needed the sunlight to grow died out. The very large animals that depended on plants to eat died out also. A few of them mangaged to survive, and
their descendants are still around today.

Chicxulub In 1982, geologists looking for oil under the Gulf of Mexico noticed a big ring of magnetic rock that was affecting their compasses. They reported it, but no one took much notice. Three years later, scientists looking at images from satellites orbiting high above Earth's surface noticed the same ring. It is near Chicxulub [CHEEKS-uh-loob], Mexico. This huge ring is about 200 kilometers across. It's now called the Chicxulub Crater, and it is almost certainly the place where the meteorite landed that might have killed many sea plants and animals. It may have also killed the ancient dinosaurs.

Look Up! It is very possible that Earth will one day be hit by another meteorite as big as the one in Chicxulub. It would certainly change our world as we know it. But forward-thinking people could design and build a missile or other system to slam into a rock in space so that it would miss our home planet. Should we spend billions of tax dollars, euros, and yen to build a "deflector system"? The price of not doing it might be bigger than we can figure.

Now, that's wild!

73 *Tyrannosaurus*
million years ago

72 *Parasaurolophus*
million years ago

71 *Thescelosaurus*
million years ago

68 *Torosaurus*
million years ago

67 *Edmontosaurus*
million years ago

TRY THIS!

THE QUESTION:

How can dust affect the temperature?

HERE'S WHAT YOU NEED:

two big, thick books • a pencil • a thermometer
a bright reading light • plastic wrap • adhesive tape • flour

1 Place two books on a table about 30 centimeters (1 foot) apart.

2 Place a pencil on the table pointing from one book to another.

3 Set one end of the thermometer on top of the pencil, at a right angle to it.

4 Stretch a sheet of plastic wrap over the whole thing. Tape the plastic wrap to the table on both sides. Shine the light on the books, pencil, and thermometer.

5 Wait five minutes, then write down the temperature.

6 Now sprinkle some flour on the plastic wrap. Wait five more minutes. Watch the temperature.

7 Brush the flour away. Wait five minutes, then check the temperature again.

The flour is like the dust that was thrown into the atmosphere from Chicxulub 65 million years ago.

PANGAEA,
One Big World

Argentinosaurus's
[arr-jen-
TEEN-uh-
Sorr-uss]
fossil was
discovered
in guess what
country?

When you look at Earth from space, or maybe just on a globe, you will notice that Africa looks as if it could fit right into South America, just like pieces of a puzzle. It turns out, they once did fit together.

Scientists have found fossils of *Titanosaurs* [tie-TAN-uh-Sorz] in Asia, Europe, and South America. Yet these continents are separated by thousands of kilometers of ocean. Dinosaur fossils helped us discover how the land we live on moves around.

All of the land on our planet used to be fused into one gigantic piece that we now refer to as "Pangaea" [pan-JEE-uh]. That means "all the world." The entire surface, or crust, of our world is made of huge rocky slabs that we call "tectonic" [tek-TAHN-ik] plates. Tectonic means "builder." By carefully studying earthquakes, mountains, valleys, and volcanoes, scientists have figured out where one plate is bumping into another and which plates are moving in what direction.

Cenozoic Era
65
million
years ago

Before the continents began to separate and the sea started sloshing over the land, dinosaurs could walk from one tectonic plate to another. That is why we now find fossils of many of the same dinosaurs all over the world. Back then, the ocean was shallower. It covered more of Earth's surface, so the Earth could hold more heat from the Sun. This warmth helped more plants grow, so there was more food around for dinosaurs to eat.

Millions of years later, after Pangaea broke up →

One continent: Pangaea →

The hot magma that is constantly churning around inside the Earth made Pangaea break apart. It took humans about a million years to figure out that we're walking around on slowly, slowly moving gigantic plates of land. By the way, South America is still moving away from Africa at about 1.2 centimeters (½ inch) a year. That's not too fast, but in a few million years, where do you think your hometown will end up?

CHECK IT OUT!

Earth still was just one big continent during the Triassic Period. It wasn't until 206–146 million years ago, during the Jurassic Period, that the continents started to spread out.

Try this. You'll have the whole world in your pan.

TRY THIS!

THE QUESTION:

What makes continental plates move?

HERE'S WHAT YOU NEED:

waxed paper • a thin metal pie pan • a microwave oven or teakettle
a coffee mug • a dinner plate • some water • food coloring • an adult

1 Cut two or three continents out of waxed paper in any shape
you like—just keep them small, about 3 centimeters
(1¼ inches) across.

2 Fill a metal pan with about 1 centimeter (⅜ inch) of cool water.
Place your continents on the surface of the water.

3 Ask an adult to help you boil 350 ml (1½ cups) of water.

4 Place the coffee mug in the middle of the plate. Pour the hot
water in the mug until it just overflows.

5 Put the pie pan on top of the hot cup. Your continents will be
driven to drift apart slowly by the heat under the pan. Put a
couple of drops of food coloring near the middle and along the
edge.

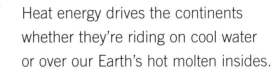

Heat energy drives the continents
whether they're riding on cool water
or over our Earth's hot molten insides.

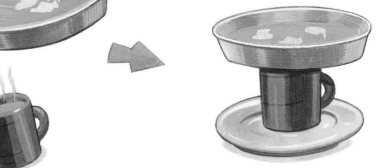

Were Dinosaurs LIKE US, or NOT?

Deinonychus [Dye-NAHN-ih-kuss] wasn't too big, compared to some of his peers, at only five feet tall—but his long, sharp, curved claws made him dangerous.

In many ways, ancient dinosaurs were nothing like us. Many of them had scaly skin or feathers. Their offspring hatched out of eggs. In other ways, dinosaurs were a lot like us. They breathed air, ran around on land, and hung out with others of their own kind. Also, they must have had ways to communicate, as the birds of today do.

Some ancient dinosaurs, like *Parasaurolophus* [pair-uh-Sorr-uh-LAH-fuss], had huge hollow spaces in their heads. Maybe they were for making trumpeting sounds. That would be like carrying about 10 extra kilograms (20 punds) around on top of their heads just to communicate with one another.

That's two watermelons' worth!

CHECK IT

OUT!

Paleontologists digging in the Patagonian desert of Argentina unearthed a nearly complete dinosaur nesting site. This amazing find revealed not only well-preserved eggs with the remains of dinosaur babies in them but also the imprint of young dinosaur skin.

LIKE US, OR NOT?
CHECKLIST OF SCIENCE

Did / Do . . .	Ancient Dinosaurs	Modern Humans
they live on land?	YES	YES
they breathe air?	YES	YES
they have scaly skin?	YES	NO
they have feathers?	YES	NO
they have hair?	NO	YES
their mothers make milk?	NO	YES
they lay eggs?	YES	NO
Were/Are they warm-blooded?	?	YES
Were/Are they cold-blooded?	?	NO

Some dinosaurs lived in family groups, as we do. Scientists figured this out when they discovered groups of nests full of fossil dinosaur eggs. We can get a good estimate of how big mother and dad dinosaurs were by measuring the distance between their nests. Ancient dinosaurs, like modern birds, must have needed enough room to move around between nests without thwapping neighbor nests with their tails. In general, the distance between nests is about the same as the length of the animal. We learned this by observing modern birds like penguins.

Some modern birds live together in big bird neighborhoods we call rookeries. That's where birds raise their offspring. It looks like some ancient dinosaurs raised their babies the same way.

TRY THIS!

THE QUESTION:

How did dinosaurs communicate?

HERE'S WHAT YOU NEED:

an assortment of plastic soda or water bottles
(try a ½-liter, a 1-liter, and three 2-liter bottles) • scissors • an adult

1 Put your mouth right up to the edge of the ½-liter bottle.
Blow gently across the top, the way a flute player makes music.
Try it with each bottle.

2 Cut the bottom off one of the 2-liter bottles and the
top off the other 2-liter bottle. Tape them together, and
you've got a double-long dinosaur head. Try blowing
across the top again. The longer the bottle, the lower
the sound you'll make.

3 Now try humming through your nose while you
blow through your mouth. Make your own dinosaur
communication sounds.

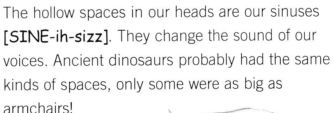

The hollow spaces in our heads are our sinuses
[SINE-ih-sizz]. They change the sound of our
voices. Ancient dinosaurs probably had the same
kinds of spaces, only some were as big as
armchairs!

from ancient DINOSAUR to Bird

Camptosaurus [Kamp-tuh-SORR-uss] was pretty flexible. He or she could walk on two or four legs, and also had a horned beak.

Scientists today are pretty sure that birds came from the theropod dinosaurs. They figured this out by comparing the shapes of bones of ancient birds like *Archaeopteryx* [Ar-kee-AHP-ter-iks] with the fossils of ancient theropods like *Velociraptors*. These animals all had S-shaped necks. They walked on two legs with three big toes pointing forward. Their leg bones were set up so that their knees were always bent as they walked.

Some theropods also had fibers or thin plates that stuck out from their skin like the teeth of a comb. Some even had feathers like those of our modern birds.

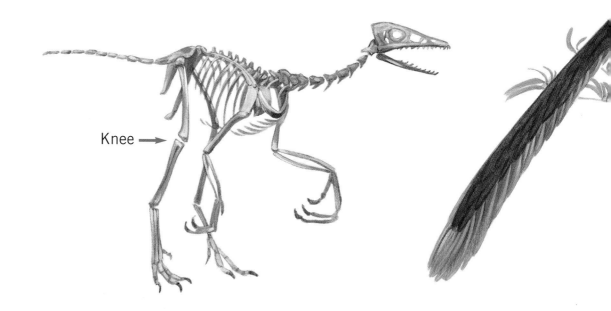

Knee →

CHECK IT

OUT!

Birds that can fly have feathers that are almost straight on the front edge and curved on the back edge, like a kayak paddle. When scientists find feather fossils, they check the edges (if they can find them) to get an idea of whether or not the animal they are investigating could fly.

We stand with our knees straight. Well, we're not theropods.

It Could Be in Their Genes There are still many things about the ancient dinosaurs that we don't know, but maybe there is a way to find out. Your body is made of tiny compartments called cells. Those dinosaurs also had cells (like birds and reptiles). In almost every cell, there are long molecules called deoxyribonucleic acid [dee-Ok-see-RIE-boe-new-KLAY-ik ASS-id], or DNA. The bundles of DNA are what we call our "genes" [jeenz]. DNA molecules are two strands of complex chemicals wrapped together, like a twisted ladder. The twisted shape of each "rail" on the ladder is called a helix [HEE-liks]. Together, the strands are called a double helix. These molecules provide all the information needed to make an animal, plant, or dinosaur. It may be possible to figure out which part of an animal's genes determine whether she or he has a heart that can pump warm blood around.

It's long been thought that if we could get hold of dinosaur DNA, we could know exactly what a dinosaur looked like. Mosquitoes existed during the period dinosaurs were around, and they bit them, just as they bite humans now. Scientists have extracted pieces of DNA from insects trapped in ancient tree sap. But the pieces are still incomplete. There could be other ways to extract dinosaur DNA. Maybe you'll figure one of them out.

TRY THIS!

THE QUESTION:

Just how long is a DNA molecule?

HERE'S WHAT YOU NEED:

two rolls of different colored crepe paper • colored pens
a big room • a globe

1 Roll out both rolls of crepe paper. Using different colored pens, write along the length of each of them a description of all the characteristics that a DNA molecule would tell you about a dinosaur—"really tall, scaly skin, big claws, long tail, carnivore, warm-blooded," etc.

2 Twist your rolls of crepe paper into a double helix.

3 Hang your twisted-paper DNA molecule from one side of a room to the other.

4 DNA is about 500 million times as long as it is wide. Your model would have to stretch 22,000 kilometers (14,000 miles), a little over halfway around the globe!

It takes a lot of genetic information to make an animal like you or a Camptosaurus.

Ancient Dinosaur Index

Allosaurus [AL-uh-Sorr-uss]: "different lizard"
9 meters (20 feet) long, 2.5 tons,
saurischian

Ankylosaurus [ang-KYLE-uh-Sorr-uss]: "armored lizard"
7 meters (23 feet) long, 1.7 tons,
ornithischian

Apatosaurus (formerly Brontosaurus) [Ah-Pah-tuh-SORR-uss]:
"deceptive lizard"
25 meters (80 feet) long, 15 tons,
saurischian

Argentinosaurus [arr-jen-TEEN-uh-Sorr-uss]:
"lizard from Argentina"
40 meters (130 feet) long, 90 tons(!),
saurischian

Brachiosaurus [BRAK-ee-uh-Sorr-uss]: "arm lizard"
26 meters (85 feet) long, 14 meters (45 feet) tall, 50 tons,
saurischian

Camptosaurus [Kamp-tuh-SORR-uss]: "bent lizard"
6 meters (20 feet) long, 1 meter (3 feet) tall, 1.5 tons,
ornithischian

Compsognathus [Komp-sahg-NA-thus]: "pretty jaw"
1 meter (3 feet) long, 3 kilograms (6.5 lbs.),
saurischian

Corythosaurus [kor-Ith-uh-SORR-uss]: "helmet lizard"
9 meters (30 feet) long, 5 tons,
ornithischian

Deinonychus [Die-NAHN-ih-kuss]:"terrible claw"
3 meters (10 feet) long, 1.5 meters (5 feet) tall,
80 kilograms (180 lbs),
saurischian

Diplodocus [Dip-LAH-dik-uss]: "double beamed"
30 meters (100 feet) long, 5 tons,
saurischian

Edmontonosaurus [ed-MUHN-tuh-Sorr-uss]:
"lizard from Edmonton, Canada"
13 meters (60 feet) long, 3.5 tons,
ornithischian

Eoraptor [Ee-oh-RAPP-ter]: "dawn (robber)"
1 meter (3 feet) long, 30 kilograms (70 lbs.),
saurischian

Giganotosaurus [jie-gan-NAH-tuh-Sorr-uss]: "gigantic lizard"
15 meters long, (50 feet), 8 tons,
saurischian

Iguanodon [Ih-GWAN-uh-Dahn]: "iguana toothed"
9 meters (30 feet) long, 5 meters (16 feet) tall, 4.5 tons,
ornithischian

Maiasaura [Mie-uh-Sorr-uh]: "good mother lizard"
9 meters (30 feet) long, 2 meters (6 feet) high, 3 tons,
ornithischian

Megalosauripus [May-gah-luh-Sorr-ih-puss]:
"great lizard foot"
height and weight unknown,
saurischian

Pachycephalosaurus [Pak-ee-SEF-uh-luh-Sorr-uss]:
"thick-headed lizard"
5 meters (16 feet) long, 1 ton,
ornithischian

Parasaurolophus [pair-uh-Sorr-uh-LAH-fuss]:
"beside Saurolophus (crested lizard)"
10 meters long (33 feet), 5 (16 feet) meters tall, 3-4 tons,
ornithischian

Plateosaurus [Platt-ee-uh-SORR-uss]: "flat lizard"
8 meters (26 feet) long, 1.5 tons,
saurischian

Scelidosaurus [SKEL-EYE-duh-SORR-uss]: "limb lizard"
4 meters (13 feet) long, 0.8 tons,
ornithischian

Seismosaurus [SIZE-muh-Sorr-us]:"quake lizard"
45 meters (150 feet) long, 15 tons,
saurischian

Thescelosaurus [THESS-eh-luh-Sorr-uss]: "marvelous lizard"
4 meters (13 feet) long, 0.3 tons,
ornithischian

Titanosaurus [Tie-TAN-uh-Sorr-uss]: "titanic lizard"
15 meters (50 feet) long, (15) tons,
saurischian

Torosaurus [TOR-uh-Sorr-uss]: "bull lizard"
7 meters (23 feet), 7.5 tons
ornithischian

Triceratops [Try-SAIR-uh-tops]:
"three-horned face"
8 meters long (26 feet), 10 tons,
ornithiscian

Tyrannosaurus rex [tih-RAN-ih-Sorr-uss]:
"tyrant lizard king"
12 meters (40 feet) long, 5–7 tons,
saurischian

Ultrasaurus [ULL-trah-Sorr-uss]:
"beyond big lizard"
17 meters (56 feet) long, 27 tons,
saurischian

Utahraptor [YEW-taw-Rapp-ter]:
"robber from Utah"
6.5 meters (21 feet), 1 ton,
saurischian

Velociraptor [veh-LAHSS-ih-Rapp-ter]: "speedy thief"
1.7 meters (5.5 feet) long, 1 meter tall,
11 kg (24 lbs),
saurischian

It sure did take us a long time to get here.

2 *human ancestors appear*
million
years ago

0.02 *humans like you*
million
years ago